ROSES FROM ASHES

FRED HUGHES

Campaign poster 1940's.

FOREWORD

How proud I felt as the Lord Mayor of Stoke-on-Trent when I attended the 70th Anniversary of the atrocities that occurred in Lidice.

When walking around the memorial site I was fascinated when people came up to me and asked me to pass on thanks to the people of Stoke-on-Trent for the help and support that they gave them in their dark days.

I also have to say how touched I was by the warm reception the Lady Mayoress and myself were given by the Children of Lidice who are now in their 80's. When I was introduced to them there were no bitter words about what had happened, but it was clear to me how much warmth they felt with our community connections and how much they were now enjoying life.

It is also gratifying to know that it was a Councillor from Stoke-on-Trent who initiated the Lidice Shall Live campaign, this being Sir Barnett Stross, a practicing GP and Councillor who later became a Member of Parliament for Stoke-on-Trent Central. On hearing of the atrocities in Lidice, together with the miners of North Staffordshire, launched a fund to ensure that Lidice would not die.

But our most poignant memory was the evening prior to the anniversary when we stood at the top of the Memorial looking down into the valley where the village once stood. Each house that made up Lidice was represented by a small light, and the Lady Mayoress and I stood there looking at the shining lights dotted around the valley, it was so peaceful and I'm not ashamed to say we both had tears in our eyes. It was a beautiful place made out of so much horror.

Councillor Terry Crowe
Lord Mayor of Stoke-on-Trent

"**The miners' lamp dispels the shadows on the coalface. It can also send a ray of light across the sea to those who struggle in darkness.**"

Barnett Stross

CONTENTS

House 56 - 58 Great Wannsee where Heydrich instigated the 'Final Solution and 'The Holocaust'.

1 BACKGROUND TO A WAR CRIME

Wannsee is a locality in the south-westernmost environs of Berlin, an attractive and modern district that holds the River Havel and incorporates two lakes with impressive forests that give the appearance of it being a virtual island. Once its seclusions provided Frederick the Great with fertile hunting parks. And, in the post-war political divisions, it was where the American occupying forces set up practice firing ranges. These days, as it has been for more than a century, Wannsee is home to exclusive golf and yacht clubs; and since the German Reunification in 1990, it has become an attractive tourist destination and a popular bathing and recreation spot for Berliners to enjoy one of the longest inland beaches in Europe.

Before the Nazis came to power in the 1930s, Wannsee attracted some of Germany's richest families who built impressive villas at the edges of its secluded forest by the blue still waters. It became a colony of millionaires living in a Mediterranean-style dream world. It was where Germany's wealthy investors and financial sponsors lived; men like Johann Hampspohn, a founding director of the modern AEG and a Reichstag delegate in the 1920s. These traditional German Protestants chose to live harmoniously alongside their upper middleclass equals including many of the country's foremost Jewish families, powerful people such as the industrialists and art patrons, Eduard and Johanna Arnhold; and Oscar Huldschinsky, another leading Berlin industrialist and arts patron. The Jewish sociologist and political economist, Franz Oppenheimer, lived here. As did the Langenscheidt publishing family, one of whose daughters, Ruth, from 1943 gave refuge to a 10-year old Jewish orphan and arranged shelter to other Jews in hiding, deeds for which she was honoured after the war.

The noted Jewish painter, Max Liebermann was one of Wannsee's more internationally known personalities. This famous proponent of French Impressionism was honorary president of the Reich's Academy of Arts before he was forced to resign in 1933, and his superb villa, a place so popular with Berlin's cultural establishment, was reduced to the status of Nazi committee rooms.

It was during 1914/15 that a German architect, Paul Baumgarten (1873-1946), built a luxurious Wannsee mansion under the commission of an affluent but eccentric pharmaceutical manufacturer, Ernst Marlier. Marlier's business, however, collapsed in 1921, and the splendid house was sold to a right-wing industrialist and financier, Friedrich Minoux. In the ever-turning wheels of fortune Minoux, in 1941, was convicted of serious fraud against the Reich and sentenced by a Nazi civil court to five years imprisonment. The house instantly came under the scrutiny of an organisation called the Stiftung Nordhav, a foundation established by the Nazi high-ranking official, Reinhardt Heydrich. The department was specifically set up to acquire real estate for the benefit of the SS Security Police and their families, and to serve as relaxation and recreation centres. But Stiftung Nordhav had a more sinister function, one that Heydrich used to build for himself a broad private property portfolio. To clear the books of suspicion, Minoux, by then languishing in Brandenburg Prison, was duly paid 1.9 million Reichmarks for the house, presumably with stolen money, and money which he never received for he died of starvation a few months after allied forces liberated him in 1945.

9

Reinhard Heydrich, author of the 'Final Solution'.

British trained Czech and Slovak commandos Jan Kubiš and Jozef Gabčík who, in collaboration with others, carried out Operation Anthropoid and the killing of Heydrich.

Although it was Heydrich's intention to use Minoux' house, 56-58 Great Wannsee, as an SS guesthouse and holiday home, he took private quarters here for himself, and it quickly became recognised as a critical centre of operations for the SS Security Service and the Reich Security Main Office.

It was at this house, on 20 January 1942, that a group of senior Nazi officials met to draft a range of policies deliberately relating to Europe's Jewish population. Reinhard Heydrich chaired this meeting from which came the order for the implementation of a policy that carried the hideous euphemism 'the Final Solution of the Jewish question'. It was at this conference that the Holocaust in the name of Operation Heydrich, a grotesque action of medieval proportions, was triggered. This depraved, unspeakable strategy began in the summer of that year with the systematic extermination of Jews, although hundreds of thousands had, by that time, already been executed by SS death squads and in odious pogroms. Heydrich, though, never lived to see the consequences of the so-called Wannsee Conference or the terrible results of the Final Solution, for he was himself executed in Prague on 27 May 1942 by British-trained Czech and Slovak commandos authorised by the Czechoslovakian government-in-exile who ordered his killing in a military style act, code named Operation Anthropoid.

The killing of one of Hitler's closest adjutants prompted the Fuhrer's lust for revenge, and a search for scapegoats was initiated with Nazi Intelligence misleadingly linking Heydrich's killing to the Czech villages of Lidice and Ležáky. For centuries Lidice had been an average agricultural village belonging to the Buštehrad manor, located in a shallow valley of the Lidice Creek in the Kladno district some 20 km west of Prague. And so, during the night of 9 June 1942, squadrons of the Nazi SS terror groups directed by RuSHA (SS Race and Settlement Main Office), an organisation responsible for 'safeguarding racial purity' in Nazi Germany, encircled the village of Lidice, blocking all potential avenues of escape to its citizens.

On 10 June, all 172 men over 15 years of age from the village were shot dead in batches of ten. Another 11 men who were not in the village were arrested and executed soon afterwards along with several others already under arrest. Simultaneously a total of 203 women and 105 children were imprisoned in the village school where the children were separated from their mothers, after which some women were taken to Prague and shot out of hand. On 12 June 1942, 195 women of Lidice were loaded onto trucks, driven to Kladno railway station and deported to concentration camps. *'By the evening of 10 June not a living inhabitant remained in the village. The men were thrown into a common grave; the houses first plundered and then burned. When only empty shells remained standing, they were demolished so that not one stone should remain on another. The rubble was cleared away, the ground ploughed up and surrounded by barbed wire fence to remain forever a barren waste as a warning to the Czechs.'*[1]

It was as though Lidice had never existed.

11

Lidice photographed before 1942 and the same scene following its destruction.

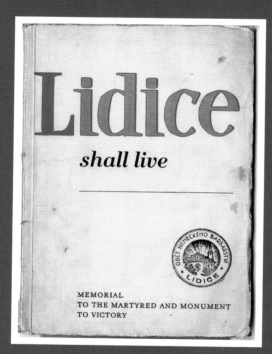

Cover of commemorative book recording the
history of the war crime.

When the war ended, 143 Lidice women were repatriated. And after a two-year search just 17 children were reunited with their mothers.[2]

There can be no doubt, though, that the instructions to the SS units that carried out this war crime had been handed down directly at the command of Adolf Hitler, who proclaimed that 'Lidice shall Die!' Moreover, it was a crime that was reported across Germany and Czechoslovakia in the headlines of the newspaper, Der Neue Tag (The New Day) on 11 June 1942:

"During the search for the murderer of SS Obergruppenfuehrer of the S.S. Heydrich, it was incontestably proved that the inhabitants of the village of Lidice, near Kladno, were aiding and abetting the perpetrators of the crime. This has been proven in spite of the fact that the population denies any such assistance. The attitude of the population in regard to such crimes is also evidenced by other hostile acts against the Reich. There were discovered, for instance, subversive literature, stores of arms and ammunition, as well as the existence of a radio transmitter and a large quantity of rationed goods held in unlawful possession. The entire adult male population was executed by firing squads. Women were deported to concentration camps and children were sent to proper places for their further upbringing. All buildings in this village were levelled to the ground and the name of the village was done away with."[3]

No one could deny that this was a crime against the civilian population; no one could refute its malicious reasoning. For here were the Nazi's own words; words that condemned them from their own mouths. It was evidence that was incontestable, evidence that had, in 1942, reached the newspapers of the allied powers across the world in words measured to convey the perfunctory retribution in perverted Nazi law. And it was that sentence underwritten by a pitiless ruling from a criminal dictator - 'Lidice will die forever', that stirred a Stoke-on-Trent general medical practitioner to proclaim in equally unwavering words, a direct response to Hitler's arrogance; an assertion that still echoes in time across seven decades - 'Lidice Shall Live'.

13

[2] Official transcription of the Trial of Major War Criminals before the International Military Tribunal Nuremberg, 14 November 1945 - 1 October 1946, et al
[3] Ibid, Trial of the Major War Criminals

Pabianice, Poland, birthplace of Barnett Stross.

Barnett Stross's mother Cecilia.
Picture by permission of Sarah Curtis

Father Samuel.
Picture by permission of Sarah Curtis

2 SETTLEMENT IN THE POTTERIES

Barnett Stross was born to a Jewish family, said originally to have the name of Strasberg, but this is not confirmed.[4] His hometown was Pabianice, the second largest town in the Lodz district of Poland. Although records of this district date back to the early 14th century, it was the empirical divisions drawn up by the 1815 Congress of Vienna that identified Poland as a client state of the Russian Empire, an enactment that triggered the region's industrialisation. By 1820 Lodz had been transformed into a well-populated centre, and the doors to Jewish immigrant workers were thrown open to the daily arrival of families from far-flung regions of Europe, including Southern Germany, Silesia and Bohemia. Indeed, by 1939 the Jewish population of Lodz numbered about 233,000, roughly one-third of the district's population.

A number of siblings preceded the birth of Barnett Stross on Christmas Day in the last year of the 19th century, 25 December 1899; an important day in the Christian calendar, but evidently a date with less meaning for a family of the Jewish faith. His parents were Samuel and Cecilia. His mother was said to have been the daughter of a Rabbi, or at least an intellectual leader of a community. They were married in 1880 and they had eleven children all of whom lived to be adults. In or about 1902 the family moved to England where Samuel, a prosperous wool merchant, had some trading connections. With his oldest sons he set up production again in the town of Dewsbury in Yorkshire. The youngest child, a daughter Ruth, was born in 1906, but this happy event was offset in 1909 by the death of Samuel which meant the older family members were left to run the business and to support their mother in bringing up the younger ones.

A year later, in 1910, Stross became a pupil of Leeds Grammar School where, listed in its alumni, are a number of notable civic leaders, several principal religious persons, and latterly such diverse former pupils such as Sir Gerald Kaufman MP, the professional golfer, Colin Montgomerie, the broadcaster and comedy writer, Barry Cryer, and Ricky Wilson, the lead singer of the Kaiser Chiefs pop band.

It is probable that by the end of his studies at Leeds Grammar School, Stross met a young art student, Olive Reid, whom he married in 1922 while he was studying at the faculty of medicine at the University of Leeds. Unsurprisingly there was some opposition to the marriage, not only because they were both very young, but also because Olive wasn't Jewish. Nevertheless, it proved to be an enduring relationship, and it was likely that she was partly the inspiration for Stross's lifelong interest in art. Olive was a woman of the Jazz Age; even in later years she was visually identifiable as a woman of the 1920s, unremarkable in appearance except that she retained 'that twenties look' and always fashioned her hair in 'the twenties bob.' Mrs. Sarah Curtis, a daughter of Stross's sister, Ruth, remembers her aunt *"as a witty and outspoken woman who had always been a perfect foil for Uncle Bob."*[5] They had no children; and in 1961 Olive died. In 1963 he remarried, to a friend with similar interests in art and philosophy, a socialist and a child psychologist, Gwen Chesters.

15

[4] Interview Sarah Curtis 26.7.12
[5] Interview Sarah Curtis 2012

The young Jewish student qualified as a doctor in 1926 with special interests in respiratory illnesses. This was possibly instinctive for someone who had grown up among factories and had firsthand experience of the chest illnesses suffered by miners in the Yorkshire coalfields and the ailments of workers in wool processing factories. Although finding a place to practice as a GP often meant graduates had to move to other regions, it quite possibly came as no surprise to his family and to Olive, that he set up in one of the most industrially polluted and blighted regions on God's Earth; a place where men and women struggled daily to catch their breath even to manage to put one foot in front of another just to make their way to hellish dust-filled potbanks, the fearsome ironworks and the black pits of North Staffordshire's coalmines. It was in this crucible of smoke and furnace-flame that Stross, in 1927, opened his surgery in a modest townhouse at the bottom of Snow Hill known as Richmond House, a community hub surrounded by the bleak works of the Cauldon Potteries, the massive Bedford Works and the monstrous Hanley gasworks.

Of course this entire landscape has changed; industry has left and Richmond House has been demolished and replaced by a modern Stoke-on-Trent College annex. In the 1920s and 30s, though, it was Satanic with few redeeming features, except one, and that came with the proximity of the Cauldon Canal, a waterway that he fell entirely in love with, employing its towpaths to walk many miles to get beyond the smoke and grime and into the beautiful countryside that leads to Leek and the Moorlands.

His zeal for canals travelled with him throughout his life; it was a pursuit to which he contributed a substantial amount of his own money for their maintenance and conservation during long periods of neglect under the ownership of the railway companies. In 1948 after the railways were nationalised, a newly created British Transport Commission oversaw the implementation of the Transport Act 1962, and the establishment of British Waterways. Barnett Stross, by then a Member of Parliament, was very much involved in this enactment throughout the committee stages.

Long before this, though, Shelton's new GP was settling down and getting to know his community of potters and miners. Soon everyone knew him as 'Doctor Bob', a man with a reputation of being a friend of working class families, a generous man who always gave his service for free if his patients were unable to pay, and in the Potteries this was often the going rate.

Within two years the seriousness of the prevalent lung disease and chest ailments that his patients were bringing to his surgery on a daily basis had made a big impression on him. He was treating men and women who were crippled with chronic respiratory diseases such as silicosis and pneumoconiosis, realising only too well that medicine could only alleviate their complaints and that he was unable to cure them of what was fearfully known as 'Potters Rot'. The impact of necessity, and the detailed knowledge of respiratory illnesses that he was continuously acquiring, attracted the attention of local trade union leaders, men like Sam Clowes, Hanley's Member of Parliament and a pivotal pottery workers' campaigner for cleaner and safer factory conditions. Clowes and his colleagues took to Stross immediately, and in turn he placed himself at the service of the Pottery Workers' Union and the Miners Federation as a medical witness who was regularly called to support their health and safety campaigns and to give evidence in compensation claims on behalf of the union members. This led to him appearing before a government committee set up expressly to inquire into the causes of silicosis in certain industries. It was partly his solicited involvement in supporting successive government welfare schemes that assisted in the introduction of a number of factory legislative changes. He greeted success in this field unceremoniously. But his modesty did not go unnoticed by trade unions and legal representatives who commended his work in a process that later became standard tribunal practice.

Busy as he was, though, Stross also found time to visit local collieries to give advice on safety measures in protecting miners from the inhalation of dust and to offer advice on underground gas awareness for which his contributions were valued by each side, by the owners as well as unions officials and workers.

In 1930 Stross joined the local Labour Party, and was soon being encouraged to stand as a councillor steered by a local party activist, Frederick Victor Saunders, who later became his parliamentary office manager. Irresistibly persuaded, he stood in the Stoke-on-Trent Council elections of 1935 and was elected to represent his home territory, the Shelton Ward 13. Stross was, by all accounts, a moderate left wing socialist, and would have been eligible for re-election in November 1939, by which time, though, the Second World War had started and he was, instead, created an alderman, a position that would keep him on the Labour benches and free from the election process for a period of nine years.

17

Snow Hill, Shelton where Stross lived at Richmond House.

The White House, Broad Street, Hanley, now the site of Mitchell Arts Centre.

Witnessing the effects of the 1930s worldwide financial and economic depression, Stross saw in person the hardships endured by poor families. He believed passionately that education for the masses was an important key to social equality, and he made this central to his political aspirations. He had been involved in extramural education almost as soon as he settled in the Potteries, giving lectures to adult learners whose formal education ended at the age of 13. He had noted that their leisure time was as aimless as the monotonous work they did, and so chose to address them at the Workers Educational Association at Longton's Sutherland Institute and classes in Newcastle-under-Lyme.

Stross and one of the WEA founders, Richard Henry Tawney, (1880-1962) became good friends. The English economics historian, social critic, ethical socialist, and educational radical, chose the Sutherland Institute at Longton to introduce the WEA to North Staffordshire in 1908. Indeed it was Stross who later helped to organise a reunion in 1951 in Longton, a reunion that gathered together Professor Tawney and that first class at the Sutherland Institute that pioneered the WEA locally.

Early picture of Barnett Stross at the time he became Member of
Parliament for Stoke-on-Trent Central.
Picture by permission of Sarah Curtis

3 THE THREAT ON THE DOORSTEP

The Stross family had left Poland to escape the 19-century Russian pogroms. And now similar Nazi activities against Europe's populations were ominously drawing World War II closer to his new home. By 1939 Stross was already involved in the resettlement of betrayed Czechoslovakian nationals, and was active with a Czech Jewish refugee, Hans Strasser, who had escaped the Nazi persecutions that were common in Germany since Hitler's rise to power in 1934. At the outbreak of war, mistreatment of Jewish communities spread rapidly into subjugated Eastern European nations. Two English human rights activists, Stephen Swingler and his wife, Anne, a vivacious left wing idealist from the slums of Newcastle upon Tyne, had befriended Strasser. These three had met in the interests of mutual aid to help the resettlement of Czech refugees; and in turn Strasser introduced his friends to the Shelton GP, and also to a supportive Stoke-on-Trent City Councillor, Charles Austin Brook, an accountant and a neighbour of Strasser in Waterloo Road, Cobridge, Stoke-on-Trent. A Yorkshire man by birth, Brook was a graduate of Cambridge, and like Barnett Stross had chosen the industrial Midlands to practice his profession. He had served as a City councilor since 1921 specialising in local government finance and education. The relationship between Stross and Austin Brook grew closer when the two later conceived the idea of the Mitchell Memorial Youth Centre in Hanley.

Anne Swingler was an important figure in the resettlement of Czech refugees. She left school at the age of 14 and took a secretarial course with the WEA, which led to a job at the Labour Research Department. Like Stross she was passionate about adult education, and she herself became a part-time lecturer in community responsibility. An active supporter of trade unions she joined the front line of the thirties hunger marches and was present during a number of London strikes and campaigns to defeat the British Union of Fascists leader, Oswald Mosley. In 1935, at the age of 20, Anne travelled alone through Nazi Germany, returning with accounts of anti-Semitism and the one-party threat to Europe's democracies. It was whilst working at Labour's Research Department in 1936, that she met Oxford student, Stephen Swingler. They came together through their political affiliations, and within months they were married.[6] It wasn't until 1937, however, that Stephen joined the Labour Party and the young couple came to live in North Staffordshire where they both were tutors for the WEA.

The Swingler's and Hans Strasser, formerly Hastra, fashioned a local branch of the Anglo-Czech Friendship Club, an organisation established to relocate the increasing number of refugees fleeing the terror of Nazism; and Barnett Stross, with his own connections with Eastern European refugees, became a natural partner.[7]

21

[6] The Guardian 11 May 2011
[7] Recollections of Charles Strasser 'From Refugee to OBE' 2007

Lord Mayor Charles Austin Brook, 1942.

Hans Strasser, co-founder of the Anglo-Czech Friendship Club.
Picture by permission of Charles Strasser OBE

Stephen Swingler MP and wife Anne, co-founder of the Anglo-Czech Friendship Club.

Throughout all of this he continued with his medical practice in Shelton, now living in a house closer to the centre of the city in Broad Street. Known as the White House because of its former painted exterior, the site where it stood is these days occupied by The Mitchell Art Centre. He also managed to carry on with his work for potters and miners, never missing an opportunity to raise medical issues inside the council with a sympathetic chief medical officer for health and an equally aligned board of governors of the North Staffs Royal Infirmary.

The Ministry of Food also sought his expert knowledge during the Second World War in which he participated by giving healthy lifestyle lectures up and down the country to workers in factories as well as organised community groups gathered in packed works canteens and village halls where wives and mothers paid attention to his recipes for healthy living. Somehow in all this he managed to attend most of his council meetings where, in the months leading up to the war, he publicly warned about the dangers of appeasement with Hitler. This brought him into discord with local Member of Parliament, Andrew MacLaren, a Scottish radical who was Burslem's MP from 1922 to 1946.

As the war approached MacLaren, a decent man who was genuinely motivated by the ideology of securing a peaceful solution to the crisis, sided with Prime Minister Neville Chamberlain's appeasement route. A letter published in the local press, the Evening Sentinel, preached agreement with the Prime Minister's negotiations over Nazi Germany's annexation of the Sudetenland territory of Czechoslovakia. Although there were certainly many in the Potteries that wanted to avoid war at any cost, there were very few that were willing to associate themselves with MacLaren's sentiments, which even his local Labour Party branches turned away from.

Stross on the other hand, was particularly concerned by what he and many others saw as Britain's duplicity in kowtowing to Hitler over Czechoslovakia. In the end, of course, Chamberlain had calculated wrongly in considering that by fully accepting the German terms, a comprehensive peace agreement would have resulted. Through his familial knowledge of Jewish suppression in Greater Europe, Barnett Stross was one who was not fooled by Hitler's guile, and continuously warned that the Nazis should not be trusted. And even while MacLaren was arguing that appeasement would work and a full-scale war could be averted if more effort was put into it, Stross, Strasser and the Swinglers were continuing to help in the resettlement of Czech refugees.

23

The 'Lidice Shall Live Campaign' launched at Victoria Hall, 1942.

> **...TO REBUILD LIDICE AND RENEW THAT FAITH AND DETERMINATION, AND TO SEE THE STRUGGLE THROUGH TO THE BITTER END. TO THE GOAL WE HAVE SET OURSELVES WITH THE REST OF THE UNITED NATIONS, NAMELY VICTORY FOR HUMAN LIBERTY, FREEDOM AND DEMOCRACY, AND DEATH TO NAZISM AND FASCISM.**

Will Lawther President of the Mineworkers' Federation of Great Britain

Edvard Beneš, the second President of Czechoslovakia and leader of the Czechoslovak government-in-exile in 1942.

Arthur Baddeley, President North Staffs Miners 1942 and co-founder of Ledice Shall Live Campaign.
Picture by permission of Muriel Stoddard

Once the announcement of the destruction of Lidice on 11 June 1942 was made, the Shelton GP immediately took up arms to organise the Lidice Shall Live campaign. In this he was allied in particular with the mining communities of Great Britain who recognised workers' affiliations with their Czech counterparts. A mention of the atrocity appears in the North Staffs Miners Federation Year Book of 1942, a statement based on Barnett Stross's own public retaliation, possibly written by Arthur Baddeley, President of the North Staffs Miners Federation:

'Though it has been totally destroyed, and our brother miners have been murdered, and the women and children battered and brutally treated by the Nazis, we say this village shall be remodelled and rebuilt, and the people shall rise and live again in a new spirit of fellowship and brotherhood. The miners would say to the world at large that their comrades of Lidice would never be forgotten, and that the widows and orphans would be rescued, and that the village would be rebuilt as a lasting monument that this crime against humanity should never succeed.'

The Lidice Shall Live campaign was launched at a packed Victoria Hall, Stoke-on-Trent, on Sunday 6 September 1942. The Evening Sentinel reported that the building *'has been the scene of many noteworthy gatherings, and many famous people have spoken from its platform. But never before has the hall held an assembly so remarkable in its significance.'*[8]

Will Lawther, President of the Mineworkers' Federation of Great Britain, stood on the spacious stage of the capacity-filled Victorian amphitheatre and pledged the miners' determination:

"...to rebuild Lidice and renew that faith and determination, and to see the struggle through to the bitter end. To the goal we have set ourselves with the rest of the united nations, namely victory for human liberty, freedom and democracy, and death to Nazism and Fascism."[9]

It was an emotional event with the Czechoslovak Army Choir singing a national hymn heralding the exiled Czech President, Dr. Edvard Beneš, who took the microphone and in an emotional speech emphasized that Lidice was only one of many victims of Germany's cruelty and oppression. He said:

"In the matter of fact there have undoubtedly been a number of similar crimes committed by the agents of the Hun throughout occupied Europe. Villages have been exterminated in Norway, in Poland, in Yugoslavia, in Russia and in other countries under German rule. But in all these other cases the Germans tried to conceal their barbarous action from the outside world. In the case of Lidice on the other side the crime was coldly premeditated in all details in the German press with evident joy and satisfaction."

25

[8] Evening Sentinel 7 Sept 1942
[9] Transcript from Lidice Shall Live launch 6.9.1942

Stross visiting Lidice, 1947.
Picture by permission of Muriel Stoddard

Lidice women returning from the concentration camps, 1947.
Picture by permission of Muriel Stoddard

Stross is given a progress report on the rebuilding of the village, 1947.
Picture by permission of Muriel Stoddard

And he ended in speaking directly to the people of the Potteries by echoing the rallying cry of Barnett Stross:

"With your generous help and our collaboration, Lidice, God willing, shall really live again. And we must all stand together in order to prepare after victory has been achieved, a peace in Europe of which we could already today solemnly declare that all we are passing through, now, today, in this war will never happen again." [10]

As a consequence of the impact of this critical event at the Victoria Hall, Will Lawther authorised the making of a Government-sponsored British documentary film telling the story of Lidice and released in 1943 called The Silent Village, made by the Crown Film Unit and directed by Humphrey Jennings, one of the founders of the Mass Observation project.

Stross's unambiguous words had clearly attracted national and international interest, and by the time the war ended in 1945 the equivalent of £1m had been raised to assist in the rebuilding of what Stross promised would be the 'New Lidice'. In 1947, at the start of that long period of post war austerity, the people of the Potteries had themselves raised and contributed an amazing £32,000 to the fund that went towards building houses in the new village.

The decision of the Czechoslovak government to rebuild the village of Lidice had been made public in June 1945 commencing with the launch of an architectural competition. In 1947 the reconstruction began with the erection of 150 detached houses for the women survivors of the 1942 atrocity who had returned from the concentration camps. The project included a community centre, a museum and a shopping centre; and there is no doubt that the money raised by the Lidice Shall Live movement contributed immensely to the results. It was Barnett Stross's involvement and his name that impressed the people of Czechoslovakia, so much so that they never forgot him. He was invited to visit, and indeed visited, Lidice several times in the post war years. And he took the lead again in 1954 when he initiated the construction of the world's largest rose garden organising the donation of 23,000 roses from 32 countries across the world. The Friendship and Peace Rose Garden was an oasis that connected the site of the destroyed Lidice and the new Lidice; and Stross was there, proudly present at its opening in 1955. In his plea for contributions, he called it, *"A fragrant symbol of the need for all nations of the world to live together in peace and friendship"*. Here Stross' name is preserved in a quiet tree-lined avenue leading to the Lidice Memorial, the Alley of Dr Barnett Stross.

In June 1947 Dr Barnett Stross MP led a delegation to Czechoslovakia at the invitation of the Czech government during which he and the leader of the miners in 1942, Arthur Baddeley, were presented with the White Lion of Czechoslovakia, the highest award the Czech nation can make to non-Czech recipients. The party consisted of civic and mining representatives including miners' leaders Will Lawther, Harold Lockett, Lord Mayor of Stoke-on-Trent, Harry Leason and Lord Mayor of the blitzed City of Coventry, Mr J Briggs.

27

[10] Lidice Shall Live, ibid

Delegates of the Miners' Union in Lidice in 1947
including National President Will Lawther and local
representatives President Harold Lockett and former
President Arthur Baddeley.
Picture by permission of Muriel Stoddard

Part of the official party that visited Lidice in 1947, during a visit to Prague.
Picture by permission of Muriel Stoddard

4 POLITICS AND ART

It was inevitable that Barnett Stross would become a politician. Whilst his medical practice took him into the social politics of community happiness and wellbeing, it has to be a matter of conjecture, however, whether he would have been a politician had it not been for the dominant socialist forces around him. The 1930s was a decade when the council sought to consolidate the plans of the Federation of 1910 and Stoke-on-Trent's elevation to the status of City in 1925. The times when philanthropy determined the politics of local government administration were passing; civic procedure was moving away from the leadership of a non-political chair directed by the Lord Mayor, and civic policies were now being maneuvered by the leader of the largest party group. The philanthropists were giving way to politicians, and in Stoke-on-Trent the politics were the politics of the working classes and those they elected to represent them from their ranks.

His first encounters with such men no doubt stemmed from the 1930s as he witnessed a drive to social equality and a comprehensive overall in education for children. He saw firsthand the leadership of men like George Herbert Barber, a man who generated social improvement based on ground level motivation rather than top down patronage. Here now were new businessmen and women whose leadership found force and acknowledgement in community development. But there was no doubt that the benchmark in the application of union politics and local government organisation was Arthur Hollins, the general secretary of the North Staffs Pottery Workers Union 1928-1946.

Hollins was, quite possibly, Stoke-on-Trent's first complete working class politician. When the two first met, Hollins had been a city councilor since 1919 and an alderman since 1928. 1928 was the year Hollins became the Member of Parliament for Hanley following in the footsteps of his trade union friend and union predecessor, Samuel Clowes. If Stross had a political mentor it was more than likely to have been Hollins, who also became Lord Mayor in 1933. Imagine the situation today - Hollins, a former factory floor pottery operative who, in that single year of 1933 held the offices of Member of Parliament, Lord Mayor, and leader of the Pottery Workers' Trade Union: how could Stross fail to be influenced by such a man.

Hollins's less well-known Labour MP colleague, at the same time sitting in the adjacent seat of Stoke, was Lady Cynthia Mosley, the wife of Oswald Mosley, who was also a Labour MP for Smethwick during the same period. Lady Cynthia was elected in 1929, although it seems that she was less active than Hollins and their Burslem equivalent, the radical Andrew MacLaren; and she certainly had very little association with Stoke-on-Trent City Council during this period. Both Lady Cynthia and her husband were supporters of Labour's first Prime Minister, Ramsay MacDonald. It wasn't long, though, before Oswald Mosley found both Labour and Conservative parties unsuitable for his needs. The Mosley's both quit Labour to form a group based on Italy's National Fascist Party. He named it the 'New Party', a quasi-military faction firmly disciplined to adopt individual unelected leadership.

During speeches at Lidice 1947, Olive Stross immediately left, Barnett Stross third from the left.
Picture by permission of Muriel Stoddard

Stross speaking in Lidice, 1955.

Barnett Stross awarded Citizenship of Lidice in 1957.
Picture by permission of Lidice Foundation

In the election of 1931, Lady Cynthia Mosley defended her Stoke seat as the New Party candidate and lost; she lost not to Labour, but to the Conservative candidate, Ida Copeland. A troubling feature of this election was that Cynthia Mosley had in fact retained a sizable core of followers in Longton where she polled 10,534 votes even though she finished behind Labour. And this particularly troubled Barnett Stross.

Continental Europe's turn to Nationalism and Fascism certainly alerted him to the dangers of the insecurities of state boundaries created by the Versailles Treaty following the Great War. And the omens sent out by Mosley and his latest movement, the British Union of Fascists (BUF), launched in 1932, was a worrying aspect in the way politics was changing, influenced by a catastrophic economic climate.

Aside from the Lidice campaign surprisingly little is known of Stross's political activities while serving on Stoke-on-Trent City Council. In 1940, however, he put his name to the launch of an appeal by his friend, Councillor Charles Austin Brook, to set up a fund to commemorate the life of Stoke-on-Trent's designer of the Spitfire fighter plane, Reginald J Mitchell CBE. He took this to a personal level when, in 1943, he gave further support by offering several of his collection of paintings for auction to promote the fund now officially endorsed by Brook who was the City's Lord Mayor that year. It was only when the war ended that the council realised just how much two world wars had delayed many of the grand plans the councillors from 1910 had set out to deliver, particularly in the arts and community culture. And now they got down to the business of reconstructing Stoke-on-Trent.

In the 30s and 40s Stross's passion for art was already well known. He had worked closely with fellow councillor, Alderman Horace Barks, in the development of libraries and in the cultural expansion of adult education through the WEA. He had already been made a member of the national Historic Buildings Council and had helped secure the preservation of several buildings that had been declared to be important to British industrial heritage. His stature as a recognised art collector had been growing for a long time and was reflected in his wide collection of Victorian and 20th century art most of which was subsequently willed to Keele University.

His love for art also brought him friendships with many notable painters, expressionists like Jacob Kramer, (1892-1962) a Ukrainian-born Jewish artist who spent all of his working life in England and who Stross and Olive both knew from their youth in Leeds where Kramer lived for many years. Another artist friend was Michael Ayrton (1921-1975). Although much younger than Stross, the Shelton doctor often put Ayrton up as a guest at Richmond House in the 1940s and 50s where the artist was fascinated by the effects of industry on the Potteries landscape. One of his large canvases is called 'The Tip'. It depicts a marl pit situated between Snow Hill and the Bedford Works, and shows a huge central crater behind which the skyline is arraigned with bottle ovens and heaps of corralled coal with the giant canister of the gasworks rearing up above a line of workers' terraced cottages.

Lord Mayor of Stoke-on-Trent Harry Leason greeting Lord Mayor of Coventry,
J Briggs. Looking on to the left are Barnett Stross and his wife Olive.
Picture by permission of Muriel Stoddard

Muriel Stoddard, daughter of Arthur
Baddeley, proudly showing her fathers
award of the White Lion of Czechoslovakia.

This was where Stross lived, here among the waste of the Potteries; a nightmare scene that he, himself, described as: *"...a dumping ground for old shards. Beneath the crockery there is a colony of rats, for when the potters empty and tip into this hole there is often food in the way of bread mixed up with the fragments."* He took a mutual friend to see it too, the British composer and orchestra conductor, Constant Lambert, who was very troubled by the journey thinking that, *"no painter could paint such a subject and do it justice."*[11] Ayrton certainly managed that, painting it in 1946 especially for Stross. It can, today, be viewed in the collections of the Potteries Museum and Art Gallery. And it is thanks to Barnett Stross that many important pieces have been gained for the benefit of the district, including a collection of the early work of LS Lowry. As well as donating many of his collections to the Lidice Foundation, he also encouraged many of his artist friends to donate their work to the Foundation as well, a treasure which today contains 433 works of art by 331 artists from 34 countries having been on display at the Lidice Gallery since 2003.

As soon as Stross entered the House of Commons in 1945, he became a co-founder of the Arts & Amenities Group of the Parliamentary Labour Party, a leading role from where he stimulated politicians on all sides of the political range to take part. His support to retain threatened collections was inspiring. In 1962 the Leonardo da Vinci cartoon of The Virgin and Child with St Anne and St John the Baptist, a privately owned work housed at the Royal Academy, was put on sale for £800,000. Amid fears that it would find its way oversees, Barnett Stross aided a campaign to keep it in England speaking passionately to a full House of Commons chamber. The famous work was exhibited in the National Gallery and visited by more than 250,000 people and donors over a four months period. And all these efforts were successful, for the cartoon was saved for the nation and is now displayed prominently in the National Gallery.

33

His niece, Sarah Curtis, recalls his diverse interests as she drew closer to him through her attraction for politics and art.

"He and his wife Olive had no children of their own and I think that my interests in politics, art and literature appealed to him. Because of this he talked to me about them. As well as asking me to tea at the House of Commons and enabling me to watch a debate, he once took me to Temple Newsom Museum in Yorkshire. His analyses of a wide spectrum of art were detailed and impressed me greatly. And Uncle Bob conveyed his opinions in a very appealing speaking voice, a sort of deep baritone that suggested he also had a good singing voice. We talked over a wide range of subjects including elements of philosophy, especially theosophy and the work of Madame Blavatski, both in India and her legacy here, in which he was deeply interested."[12]

[11] The Antonine Itineraries weblog - author Antony Clayton
[12] Recollections of Sarah Curtis

Campaigning in the 1938 local election.
Picture courtesy of Don Barnes

Stross entertaining female constituents at the House of Commons.
Picture by permission of Maureen Hayward

It was in 1948 that Austin Brook's proposals for the Reginald Mitchell community initiative really started to come to fruition. This was the year when Stross moved permanently out of the White House in Broad Street, donating both property and land to the Mitchell fund. The house was demolished and the site cleared in 1950; and on 16 May 1955, Lord Mayor, Alderman Annie Longsdon Barker, laid the foundation stone for the future Mitchell Memorial Theatre and Youth Centre in the presence of Austin Brook. The theatre and youth centre, known as Cartwright House, was officially opened on 28 October 1957 by Royal Air Force fighter pilot ace, Group-Captain Douglas Bader. This iconic legacy was achieved only through the generosity of Barnett Stross, a gift of one of Hanley and Shelton's earliest professional town houses built c.1800.

Stross's political career, as previously referred to, began when he became a city councillor. It was in 1945 that the pottery workers' champion, 69-year old Arthur Hollins, chose to take retirement from his position as General Secretary of his trade union and as Member of Parliament for Hanley. Stross was persuaded to stand by the local Labour Party members, fronted by Frederick Saunders who stood as his election agent. And in reality there was no better candidate; there was no local person who enjoyed such national and international standing than the Shelton GP; and what's more he was considered to be a true native citizen of the Potteries.

He was 46 when he entered Labour's reforming parliament under the leadership of Prime Minister Clement Attlee, on 2 August 1945. He was admitted and sworn in alongside his friend and fellow freedom campaigner, Stephen Swingler, who had been elected for Stafford and later, in 1951, for Newcastle-under-Lyme. Using his background in medicine, Stross at once made an impact in debates and contributions to welfare and employment reform as well as fully enjoining in the debate over the United Nations Charter. Legislation on compensation for the diseases of silicosis and pneumoconiosis were among many successful crusades that became policy in the early years of Labour's nationalisation programme.

His attendance record was faultless and he rarely missed an opportunity to engage in any debate, or to put questions to ministers on such diverse subjects as the controversial African redevelopment schemes, and child care, national insurance and unemployment assistance, and even in making a case for the involvement of North Staffordshire in the Festival of Britain in the summer of 1951. He had by now become a Londoner living in a flat in Thorney Court, at the junction of Gloucester Road and Kensington Gore, although he kept his accommodation practice in Shelton for a further period helped out by partnerships of medical practitioners.

Alderman Horace Barks OBE, friend and colleague
of Barnett Stross, founder of Stoke-on-Trent
Libraries and Art Galleries.

Sketch of Barnett Stross by his good friend
Horace Barks OBE.
By permission of Barry Sergent

There is little doubt that he stood on the left of Labour socialists politics, and was later a self-declared and acknowledged Bevanite, a supporter of the larger-than-life post-war Minister of Health, a department that also covered social housing. It was Bevan that implemented the new and comprehensive free National Health Service and began tackling the country's desperate housing shortage, two areas that were close to the moral principles of Barnett Stross. Free health service paid for directly from public money had always been one of his aspirations. And the increase for the Welfare state expenditure by increasing marginal tax rates for the wealthy was part of what the Labour government largely saw as the redistribution of the wealth, one of Stross's early yearnings.

In the New Years Honours of 1964 he received a Knighthood; and in the October elections when Labour was returned to power, the leader and new Prime Minister, Harold Wilson, made him a Junior Minister of Health, a post created in 1919 in the reconstruction of the Local Government Board. These functions were transferred in 1968 when the department was amalgamated with Social Security and Social Services, and ultimately became the Department of Health and Social Security in 1988, which shows how important Stross was to Labour's social strategy.

37

His wife, Olive, had died just before these events came to pass. And it was his second wife, Gwen, who became Lady Stross, a dedicated companion who supported him as he gradually became ill, no doubt accentuated by the tremendous pressure he exerted while in charge of an extremely demanding and hands-on ministerial post in a government with a tiny majority. Nonetheless, Barnett Stross remained active and made his last speech in a debate on elderly care just before 10.15pm as Parliament broke up for Christmas on 16 December 1964.

Almost portentously he made a reference to his own background. In his summing up to the debate on elderly care, he told the House there were some 40,000 old people living in warden-serviced housing and that he had plans to increase this to 140,000 in the ensuing five years while constantly retaining ways to improve such services. Then he turned aside and said:

"It should not be supposed, however, that old age is itself a disability, or that 65 years represents a specific watershed, after which a man loses his capacity for helping himself or helping others. There are too many examples around us, in the House, in particular, for us to fall into error on that score. Indeed, when I recall that my birthday, on Christmas Day, will allow me to reach the age of 65, and that the great playwright Sophocles, wrote his greatest play at the age of 95, I feel extremely young and encouraged."[13]

[13] Hansard

The foundation stone at Mitchell Memorial Theatre being laid by
Lord Mayor Annie Longson Barker with Alderman Austin Brook (left).

Stross in Parliament with fellow MPs and his Parliamentary Secretary
Frederick Victor Saunders (back row).
Picture by permission of Maureen Hayward

But he wasn't well. He resigned the ministerial position on 24 February 1965, and rarely attended the House thereafter, contributing to debate just once in 1965 and once more in March 1966, days before the election that returned Wilson's Labour with an increased majority. He had already made his decision not to stand for re-election telling his constituency party in mid 1965 to look for another candidate.

His health now deteriorating fast, Barnett Stross was admitted to the University College London where he died on 14 May 1967 age 68.

In his maiden speech to the new House on 2 May 1966, Stoke-on-Trent Central's new MP, Robert Cant, paid a generous tribute to his predecessor:

"I have the very great honour of following Sir Barnett Stross and I think that both sides of the House would agree that he established himself in the hearts of everybody and made a tremendous contribution to the work of the House in the many years he was a Member. I assure honourable Members that he did this equally in Stoke-on-Trent where he not only became the medical man to a large number of lay people but the medical adviser to the pottery and mining industries and became very intimately associated with them. Therefore, in a sense I have the great advantage of basking in a little of reflected glory from Sir Barnett Stross, but at the same time I am very conscious of the very high standards which he set me, and I can only hope that I can in some measure live up to them."

Mr. Cant ended by saying: *"I hope that in the years to come I can make some sort of contribution which will commend itself to the House, and that my general conduct in the House will lead me to earn something of the respect which my predecessor, Sir Barnett Stross, obviously enjoyed."*[14]

At the funeral the Prime Minister, Harold Wilson, was represented by his Parliamentary Private Secretary, Harold Davies MP, a close friend of Barnett Stross and Labour member for the adjacent constituency of Leek. Among family mourners, principal guests included the Czech Ambassador Miloslav Růžek, his wife and Embassy staff members. The Member of Parliament for Stoke-on-Trent North, John Forrester, represented the Lord Mayor; and Robert Cant represented the citizens of Stoke-on-Trent. Leslie Sillitoe, Assistant General Secretary of the Pottery Workers' Union, attended on behalf of the union. Stephen Swingler and Anne Swingler represented the Society for British Czechoslovak Relations alongside representatives of the British Czechoslovak Friendship League and the Lidice Shall Live Committee. The Vice Chancellor of Keele University, Professor Hugh-Jones, beneficiary of the Stross Art Collection, was also at the cremation service at Hoop Lane Golders Green where Rabbi Herbert Richter conducted the service followed by an address by his very close friend, the Rt. Hon Emanuel Shinwell, MP.

[14] Hansard 3 May 1966

'The Tip' by Michael Ayrton. The view from the rear of Richmond House, Shelton, where Stross lived.

5 FAITH

Barnett Stross engaged in supporting Jewish causes, which he celebrated as often as he could whilst juggling his many work commitments and professional activities. The early memories of his time in North Staffordshire's Jewish community have been lost over the years. It was, however, a small community that was founded by 26 Jews in Hanley in 1872, a community that numbered some 200 at the time of Stross's death and continued to fall until the synagogue, a building that opened in 1922 in Birch Terrace, closed altogether in 2008. However, the Jewish community still thrives having moved to a smaller purpose-built centre in Newcastle-under-Lyme.

Stross worked closely with several leading members of North Staffordshire's Jewish community including local businessman, Colman Sumberg, who was recognised as the lay head of the community for many years. They helped to forge connections with many other elements of Stoke-on-Trent organisations and played a big part in the advancement of Stoke-on-Trent Repertory Players. Mr. J. Kay, another leading Jewish citizen was a close friend, as was Saul Simon, a city magistrate and an enthusiastic supporter of the Council for Social Services and innumerable other welfare organisations. Many, like Stross, were medical practitioners - John Jordan, the ear, nose, and throat surgeon, who had fled from Czechoslovakia, and the eminent gynæcologist, Harold Burton, were just two close associates among many medical professionals from other parts of the country.

41

In an article written for the Jewish Chronicle in 1960, Stross recalled that: *"Although some of North Staffordshire's 60 Jewish families are third generation citizens, quite a few have settled in the area as refugees from Nazism. The Hitler terror brought into the city a number of Czech, Austrian, and German families, including a group of Czech children rescued in the last hour. They were cared for by a Refugee Committee composed of Jews and Gentiles, and assisted by almost every organisation in the city."*[15]

He was, of course, referring to his associations with Hans Strasser and the Swingler's who he never failed to mention when recalling those wartime events.

[15] The Jewish Chronicle 8 April 1960 pg 10

IN 2010 OWNERS OF THE ARTBAY GALLERY IN FENTON, ALAN AND CHERYL GERRARD, BECAME THE ADMINISTRATORS OF THE CHILDREN'S ART COMPETITION WHICH HAD ALREADY BEEN RUNNING FOR MANY YEARS IN THE CZECH REPUBLIC. BELOW ARE ENTRIES FROM CHILDREN, LOCAL AND INTERNATIONAL, THAT WON RECOGNITION.

Thomas Whitaker, aged 6, Wiltshire. Private entry. Overall Primary School Winner.

Daniel Cotterill, aged 9, Blurton Primary School. Staffordshire Primary Schools County Runner Up.

6 THE FUTURE

In 1967, a year after the death of Barnett Stross, an Exhibition of children's Artistic Expressions publicised under the name, Our Childhood is Different, was shown in the Klement Gottwald Museum in Prague. Here the artistic work of children from Czech schools was exhibited, and it included literary work as well as painting, sculpture and ceramics. This led to the foundation of the International Children's Exhibition of Fine Arts opened in 1972 located at the purpose built Lidice community centre. The organisation comprises of a competition for children, and the inaugural challenge included entries from children from 15 countries, with 224 prizes being awarded to the successful entrants.

Between the time of its inception and 1990 the exhibition became truly international, reaching out to children aged from 5 to 15 years in more than 60 countries through the communication of multi-linguistic order and interconnection. Awards in the shape of medals known as 'Lidice Rose' were distributed at exhibitions at annual ceremonies in the Lidice community centre from May to October.

Between 1991 and 2004 the exhibitions were held at a number of different Czech Republic places until they returned to the Lidice Gallery in 2004, and are now organised by the Lidice Memorial, a department of the Ministry of Culture of the Czech Republic and supported by the Ministry of Education, the Youth and Sports department of the Czech Republic, the Ministry of Foreign Affairs, and the Czech Commission for UNESCO. Since September 2007 Ivona Kasalická has been the curator of the exhibition, who reported that in 2011 children from more than 60 countries had participated in the exhibition that year, contributing some 25,000 pieces of work from around the world.

In July 2010, the owners of Theartbay Gallery in Fenton, Stoke-on-Trent, Cheryl and Alan Gerrard, initiated a drive to re-establish the cultural, social and economic links between Stoke-on-Trent and Lidice. One aspect of this involves expanding an ongoing programme of presentations to local schools designed to advance closer relationships between the two communities.

In May 2011 Theartbay Gallery set up The UK Children's Fine Art Competition (UKCFAC), the largest UK contributor to the International Children's Exhibition of Fine Art (ICEFA). This is intended to give children across the UK, and beyond, an opportunity to identify and celebrate the life and work of Sir Barnett Stross, and the miners and pottery workers of North Staffordshire, whose generosity and support went so far in helping to rebuild Lidice and to make it live again.

Ian Hai, aged 4, Hong Kong. Private entry. International Winner.

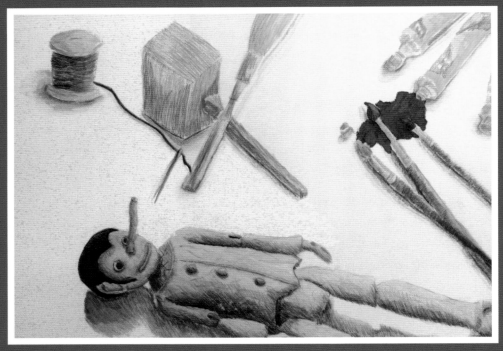

Holly Madew, aged 14, Fenton, Private entry. Staffordshire Secondary Schools County Winner.

Initial submissions of 400 pieces of art produced by Stoke-on-Trent pupils formed the basis of a pilot competition and were subsequently entered into the international exhibition - the ICEFA. The venture has since become a UK-wide event attracting in excess of 2000 exceptional entries. Significantly each participant is encouraged to learn the historical background common to both communities thereby engaging in a journey of discovery as they create their work.

In November 2010 a council-supported delegation, led by Councillor Hazel Lyth, Portfolio Holder for Culture, including Cheryl and Alan Gerrard, visited Lidice and met the Mayor of Lidice, Veronika Kellerova, and representatives of Lidice Art Gallery, to discuss possible future links with the village and Stoke-on-Trent. A delegation from the Lidice Museum responded by visiting Stoke-on-Trent later that month.

This was followed in June 2011 with a commemoration for Lidice at Albert Square, Fenton, led by Lord Mayor, Terrence Follows, and featured poetry composed by children from local schools. And in June 2012, representatives of Stoke-on-Trent City Council attended a memorial service at Lidice where wreathes were placed to commemorate the 70-anniversary of the Nazi war crime. The Lord Mayor of Stoke-on-Trent, Councillor Terry Crowe, laid a wreath on behalf of the people of Stoke-on-Trent, complemented with many more floral tributes from around the globe. Such events certainly evoke the memory of Sir Barnett Stross and the unbreakable and unforgettable links between the Czech Republic and the United Kingdom, and Lidice and Stoke-on-Trent. Links have certainly been established with schools in both countries and a number of future events are certain to be undertaken.

The legacy of Barnett Stross lies not only in the remedial comfort he brought to his patients, the miners and the pottery workers, but also in his endorsement of adult education and the promotion of global art and culture. His career in politics stemmed from his love for his adopted city, which he carried onto the stage of international fellowship. Perhaps, though, he should be remembered best of all for the astonishing way he cultivated roses from ashes.

Children from the Czech Republic visiting Stoke-on-Trent, 2012.

Barnett Stross 1899 - 1967.

Dr Barnett Stross Avenue, Lidice (Alej Dr Barnett Stross).